The Armor of God

BIBLE CHAPTERS
FOR KIDS

I can be strong during difficult times, because I have God's power with me.

"Be strong in the Lord, and in the power of His might."

God's power is like a
spiritual armor that
protects me from the
devil's temptations.

"Put on the whole armor
of God, so that you can
stand strong against
the devil's plans."

I should not fight against others that might do mean things to me, but rather against the evil and the bad.

"We don't fight against people on earth, but against the devil's kingdom."

The devil is our enemy,
but we can't see him or
strike at him physically.

"Our fight is against the
spiritual powers of evil
in the world and in the
heavens."

I have to get myself ready.
Like a great warrior of God,
I can learn how to put on a
spiritual armor to protect me.

"That's why we need to put on
the whole armor of God, so that
we may be able to stand strong
when evil comes our way."

God is strong and powerful, and He is always with me. Like a good tight belt, the truth of God's Word will support and protect me.

"So stand firm, having the belt of truth around your waist."

God teaches me to do what is right and to show kindness, even when the devil tries to pull me the other way. I guard my own heart and demonstrate that I'm strong with God's help by showing love to others.

"And on your chest, wear the breastplate of righteousness."

I am ready to go and tell others about the good news of God's love and peace.

"And on your feet, prepare yourself to walk and spread the good news of peace."

I use the shield of faith to protect myself from the devil! Faith is to trust God and believe in Him, even though I can't see Him with my eyes. God believes in me, and I believe in Him. When I trust in God, I am strong.

"By taking the shield of faith, you will be able to put out all the fiery darts of the wicked."

Jesus' sacrifice protects my soul in the same way that a helmet protects my head. God rescued me from my mistakes when Jesus died to save me.

"Take the helmet of salvation."

I can use God's Word as a powerful weapon against the devil. When I'm tempted to do something wrong, the Bible reminds me of what I should do instead.

"And take the sword of the Spirit, which is the Word of God."

Now that I have my
spiritual armor on, I
will practice using it.
I pray often and ask
Jesus to guide me.

"Always be
prayerful and ask
God for what
you need."

I need to be ready to face the devil at all times and pray that others can do so as well.

"You must always be ready and never give up. Pray often for all of God's people."

Dear God,

Please help me to put on Your armor of the spirit every day.

Help me to choose good when I am tempted to do wrong.

Teach me to

do the loving thing.

Give me boldness to tell others about You. Remind me to read and follow Your Word.

God, please make me strong in You. Amen.

a time to praise

Thank You, dear God,
that You have given me
this armor of protection
against the devil.

Thank You for giving
me strength, even when
I feel weak.

I praise You for always
being there to help me.

More books in the series:

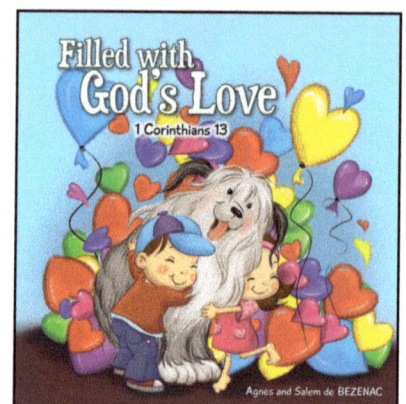

A song of **Praise**
with Psalm 100

PSALM 119

Agnes and Salem
DE BEZENAC

Agnes and Salem
de BEZENAC

SAFE WITH GOD
Psalm 91

PROVERBS

Agnes and Salem
de BEZENAC

My Shepherd Psalm 23

Filled with
God's Love
1 Corinthians 13

Agnes and Salem de BEZENAC

iCHARACTER

Published by iCharacter Ltd. (Ireland)
www.icharacter.org
By Agnes and Salem de Bezenac
Illustrated by Agnes de Bezenac
Colored by Henny
Copyright. All rights reserved.
All Bible verses adapted from the KJV.

www.ingramcontent.com/pod-product-compliance
Lightning Source LLC
Chambersburg PA
CBHW040252100426
42811CB00011B/1232